5/05

21

BIG BUBBLEFACTS

History

BIG BUBBLEFACTS

History

Miles Kelly
PUBLISHING

501341868

First published in 2005 by
Miles Kelly Publishing Ltd
Bardfield Centre, Great Bardfield, Essex, CM7 4SL

Copyright © Miles Kelly Publishing Ltd 2005

2 4 6 8 10 9 7 5 3 1

Publishing Director:
Anne Marshall

Senior Editor:
Belinda Gallagher

Editorial Assistant:
Hannah Todd

Designers:
Debbie Meekcoms
Louisa Leitao

Cartoons:
Mark Davis

Production:
Estela Boulton

ISBN 1-84236-610-6

Printed in China

British Library Cataloguing-in-Publication Data
A catalogue record for this book is available from the British Library

Indexer: Jane Parker

www.mileskelly.net
info@mileskelly.net

Contents

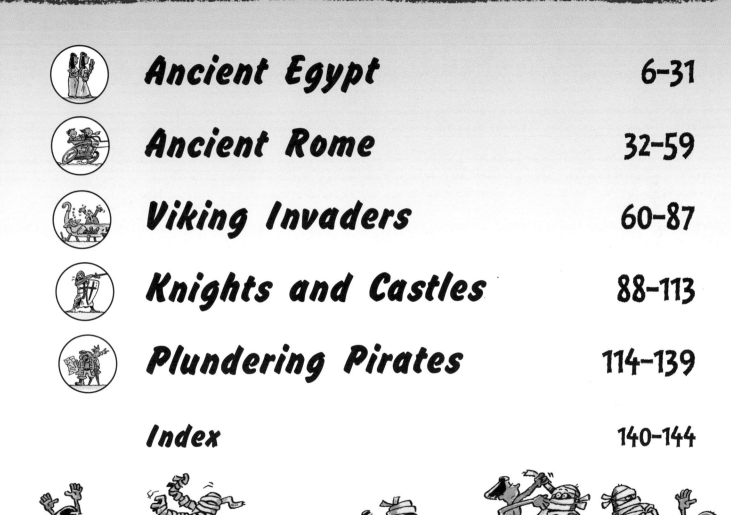

ANCIENT EGYPT

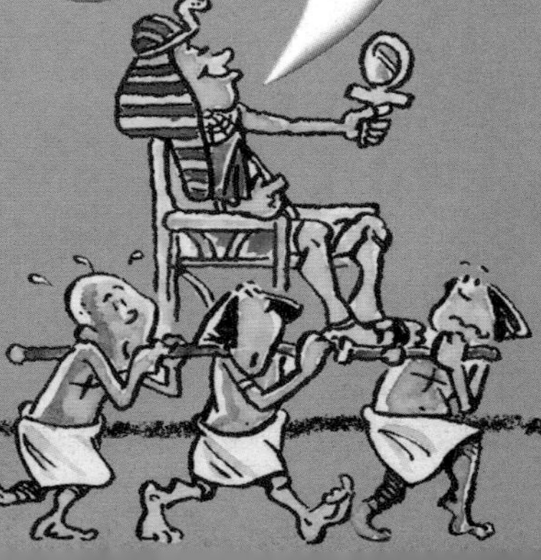

Fancy pharaohs
leaders of Egypt

Rulers of ancient Egypt were called pharaohs. The word pharaoh means 'great house' and comes from the Egyptian word for palace – *per'ao*. The pharaoh was the most important and powerful person in the land and ordinary people believed he was a god.

Can you believe it?

Women courtiers wore hair cones made of animal fat scented with spices and herbs.

THIS FEATHER IS SO HEAVY!

I QUITE FANCY NAIL EXTENSIONS.

GUCCI, ARMANI...

The pharaoh was waited on hand and foot while people came to pay him tribute. They often gave gifts.

The pharaoh had many wives and he usually married a close female relative. He had lots of children!

The eldest son of the pharaoh became the next leader. Female pharaohs were not very common!

Home sweet home
Egyptian style

Egyptian houses were made from mud bricks dried in the sun.

Mud from the River Nile was mixed with straw and pebbles to make it stronger. Tree trunks supported the flat roofs. Inside walls were plastered and painted. Wealthy Egyptians lived in large houses while a poorer family might live in a single room.

Many poor people lived in a crowded single room, but the rich had spacious villas with a walled garden.

Food was cooked in a clay oven or over an open fire. Most kitchens were equipped with a cylinder-shaped oven made from bricks of baked clay. Egyptians burned either charcoal or wood as fuel and cooked food in two-handled pottery saucepans.

Egyptians furnished their homes with wooden stools, chairs, tables, storage chests and carved beds. A low three- or four-legged footstool was one of the most popular items of furniture. Mats of woven reeds covered the floors.

The Egyptians ate with their fingers. Servants brought jugs of water so people could rinse their hands.

Baking and brewing

bread and beer!

Bread was the most important food in ancient Egypt. Grain was stored in huge granaries until it was needed. Ordinary Egyptians' favourite drink was beer. Models of brewers were even left in tombs to make sure the dead person had a plentiful supply of beer in the next world!

WHISTLE WHILE YOU... HIC... WORK!

THESE NEW PIZZA BASES ARE SELLING LIKE HOT CAKES!

ONE LARGE BLOOMER — ANYTHING ELSE MADAM?

A rough bread was made from wheat or barley. The gritty pieces often wore down people's teeth!

As well as beer, the Egyptians made wine, usually from grapes. After harvesting, the grapes were trodden by foot in a wine press, until every last drop of juice was squeezed out! The juice was then left in jars to ferment (turn into alcohol).

Beer made from barley was drunk by the poor. It was so thick it had to be strained before drinking.

Looking good!

Egyptian fashion

Egypt was a hot country so people wore cool, loose-fitting clothes. Noblewomen's dresses were made from the finest cloth with beads sewn onto it. Men wore robes or a piece of cloth worn like a kilt. Ordinary workers just wore a simple cloth tied at the waist.

Clothes were made of linen, a cloth spun from a plant called flax. Shoes were a luxury, loved by the rich!

Sandals were made from papyrus, a kind of reed. Rich people, courtiers and kings and queens wore padded leather sandals, but footwear was a luxury item, and most ordinary people walked around barefoot. Sometimes sandals were painted onto the feet of mummies!

Lucky charms called amulets were also worn. They were supposed to protect the wearer from evil spirits and bring good luck. One of the most popular ones was the eye of the god Horus. It was meant to protect everything behind it. Children wore amulets shaped like fish to protect them from drowning in the River Nile.

LOOKS LIKE STILETTOS ARE IN AGAIN.

BANG! BANG!

WHAT D'YA THINK?

YUK!

IT'S VERY... ...BRIGHT!

JUUCC

SNIP SNIP!

BLING!

Women wore long dresses while men wore kilt-like skirts. Wigs were popular with men and women!

Buying and selling
trade in Egypt

Egyptians did not use money to buy and sell goods. Instead they exchanged goods with other traders. Merchants visited the countries bordering the Mediterranean Sea as well as those lands to the south. The Egyptians offered gold, a kind of paper called papyrus, and cattle.

Can you believe it?

Fly swatters made from giraffe tails were a popular fashion item in ancient Egypt.

Egyptians traded food and goods such as linen and papyrus with Nubia, a land to the south of Egypt.

Most towns had a market and people took oil in huge pots, which they exchanged for food or cloth.

People could also buy pots and pans, animal skins, silver, copper – in fact, almost anything!

Pyramid builders

tombs of kings

The huge stones had to be levered into exactly the right position. Up to two million blocks of stone could be used to make one pyramid. Teams of workers had to drag the stones up steep slopes.

The three pyramids at Giza were built for kings Khufu, Khafre and Menkaure. Pyramids were huge burial chambers. The biggest, the Great Pyramid, took more than 20 years to build. About 4000 stonemasons were needed to complete the job.

The finished pyramids were given a white coating to protect the stones beneath

Wooden sledge for dragging the blocks of stone

The pyramids at Giza are more than 4500 years old. The Great Pyramid is about 140 metres high.

Steep ramps of earth were built
to raise the stones onto the
pyramid structure

Workers were supplied with water
while working in the hot sun

The Sphinx, a stone statue, guards the pyramids. It has the body of a lion and the head of King Khafre.

Down
on the farm
a farmer's tale!

The farming year was divided into three seasons: the flood, the growing period and the harvest. Most people worked on the land, but between July and November the land was covered by flood waters. People went off to help build pyramids and royal palaces.

CRACK!

WHO DOES HE THINK HE IS?

YEAH — IF HE CRACKS THAT WHIP AGAIN...

Farmers used wooden ploughs pulled by oxen to prepare the soil. Seeds were planted by hand.

Wheat and barley were the two main crops. At harvest time, wooden sickles were used to cut the crop.

Farmers had to hand over part of their harvest as tax payment. It was given to the local temple.

A hard day's work

scribing away!

Scribes were very important people in ancient Egypt. These highly skilled men kept records of everything that happened from day to day. Craftworkers produced statues, furniture and other goods for the pharaoh. These workers sometimes had special villages built for them, especially those who worked on the pharaohs' tombs.

A scribe wrote with a reed pen onto papyrus, a kind of paper. Scribes kept track of everything.

Only the sons of scribes could undergo the strict scribe training, which began at about nine years of age. It took years to learn the hundreds of hieroglyphs (word pictures) that were used in writing.

Craftworkers included carpenters, potters and jewellers. They worked mainly for the pharaoh.

Tombs and thieves
deep underground

From about 2150BC, the pharaohs were buried in tombs in the Valley of the Kings. The tombs were cut deep into rocks or underground. Over the years, robbers stole everything from these tombs – gold, silver, precious stones, furniture. Sometimes they even stole the body of the dead ruler.

GET ME A MUMMY!

IT'S LIKE ALADDIN'S CAVE.

THAT'S ALI BABA.

WHERE'S THE LIGHT SWITCH?

OPEN SESAME!

The entrance to the Valley of the Kings was guarded, but robbers broke into every tomb, except one.

can you believe it?

A handbook for tomb robbers, 'The Book of Buried Pearls', gave tips for sneaking past the spirits that guarded the dead!

All kinds of treasure was buried with a dead king in his tomb. It included gold, silver and precious stones along with personal belongings, jewellery and clothes. The tomb of Tutankhamun revealed the king's solid gold death mask.

The tomb of Tutankhamun, the boy king, was discovered almost untouched in 1922.

Making mummies

wrap it up!

Mummies were dead bodies that had been preserved by priests. The ancient Egyptians thought that the dead lived on in another world and that they would need their bodies in the afterlife. This meant that bodies were mummified, or dried out.

It took up to 70 days to prepare a body and only kings and nobles could afford the full treatment.

Making a mummy was a very skilled job. First of all, the internal organs such as the brain and lungs were removed. Then the body was covered in salts and left to dry for 40 days. The dried body was then stuffed with linen to help it keep its shape. Finally, the body was oiled and wrapped in layers of linen bandages.

When the body was ready for burial, the chief priest said prayers to help the dead person on their journey to the next world. He wore a jackal mask to represent Anubis – god of embalming (preparing bodies to be mummified). As jackals were often found near cemeteries, Anubis was given the form of a jackal.

GENTLY!

HOLY WATER? NO, IT'S JUST BOTTLED, I'M AFRAID!

SOB! WAIL!!

AATCHOOO!

I'M HAVING THE CAR!

The mummy of a pharaoh was sealed inside a stone coffin called a sarcophagus.

The Egyptians worshipped more than 1000 different gods and goddesses. The most important god was Ra, the Sun god. People believed that he was swallowed each evening by the sky goddess, Nut. During the night Ra travelled through the underworld and was born again in the morning.

As well as Ra, Sobek, god of the Nile, was important. Crocodiles were kept in pools near his temples.

Thoth was moon god and gave people writing. Bastet was goddess of cats, musicians and dancers.

Anubis looked after the dead, and watched over them as their bodies were made into mummies.

Heroes of Egypt...
heroines too!

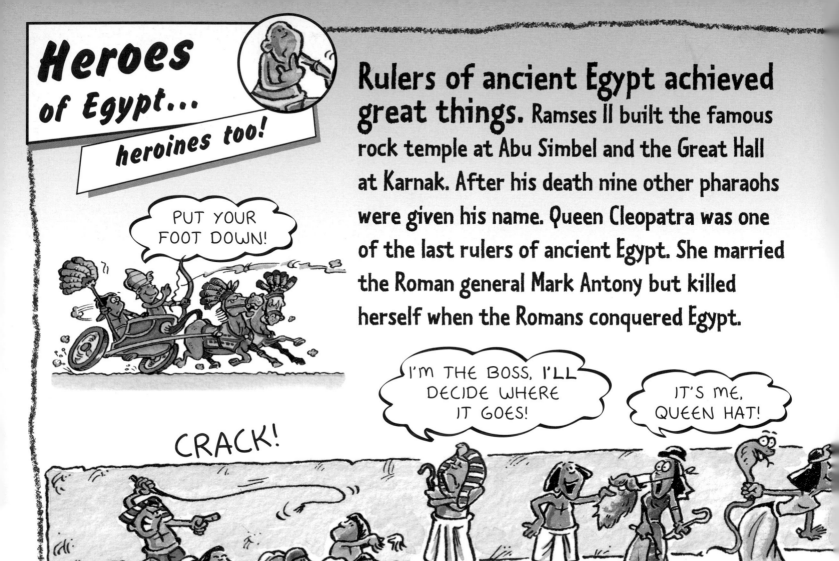

Rulers of ancient Egypt achieved great things. Ramses II built the famous rock temple at Abu Simbel and the Great Hall at Karnak. After his death nine other pharaohs were given his name. Queen Cleopatra was one of the last rulers of ancient Egypt. She married the Roman general Mark Antony but killed herself when the Romans conquered Egypt.

PUT YOUR FOOT DOWN!

I'M THE BOSS, I'LL DECIDE WHERE IT GOES!

IT'S ME, QUEEN HAT!

CRACK!

Thutmose III had a huge obelisk (stone pillar) made. It now stands by the River Thames in London.

Soldiers who fought bravely in battle were given golden fly medals for 'buzzing' the enemy so successfully!

Queen Hatsheput was often shown wearing men's clothing and a false beard. She was the wife of Thutmose II. On his death, Hatsheput took the title of pharaoh and adopted the royal symbols of the double crown, the crook, the flail (whip) – and also the ceremonial beard!

LOOK, CLEO, WHAT ABOUT CAESAR? IT'S ME OR HIM!

IT'S MY TREASURE!

I'M NOT CARRYING THIS ALL THE WAY TO LONDON...

Perhaps the most famous pharaoh is Tutankhamun, and his tomb of fabulous treasure.

ANCIENT ROME

At home in Rome

city of smells!

Rome was a dirty, stuffy place to live. Poorer people lived in blocks of flats called *insulae* and the smell must have been awful in summer! Rich people owned country homes called villas and during summer they often escaped to them to get away from the smell and heat of the city.

HE STINKS!

WHAT? DON'T LOOK AT ME!

WHAT A TERRIBLE WHIFF!

People living in *insulae* threw their waste into the street. The smell would have been unbearable!

Only the rich could afford country villas. They would leave the dirty, smelly city behind in summer.

Villas had central heating. Air was warmed by a wood furnace under the floor, kept burning by slaves.

Father knows best...

happy families

A Roman father ruled the roost! Each family was headed by a man. He was known as the *paterfamilias* (father of a family). The house and its contents belonged to him and he had the right to punish any family members who misbehaved. Even his mother and other older female relatives had to obey him.

Roman familes included everyone living and working in one household – even slaves!

Can you believe it?

Lupercalia was Valentine's Day in Rome. Boys picked a girl's name from a hat, and she was their girlfriend for the year!

Roman families liked to keep pets. Statues and paintings show many children playing with their pets. Dogs, cats and even doves were popular. Some families also kept ornamental fish and tame deer.

AHHH! HE'S SO CUTE!

HE'S UGLY!

I WILL **NOT** HAVE DOVES NESTING IN THE HOUSE.

FETCH IT BOY!

YOU FETCH IT!

Girls married at 12 years of age and most marriages were arranged – love was not considered important.

Rules of school

read, write, speak

DOESN'T HE GO ON.

Roman boys learned to speak well. Schools taught reading, maths and public speaking. Boys usually became politicians, army leaders or government officials and they all had to make speeches in public, explaining their plans. Boys went to school at seven years old and left aged 16.

TRIP UP THE WAITER!

WHAT'S THE BEST WAY TO SEE FLYING SAUCERS?

Wealthy students sometimes went to Greece to be taught public speaking by the best Greek teachers.

Students wrote on wooden tablets coated with wax. Others scratched their writing on bits of pottery.

Romans read standing up from scrolls. Scrolls were 10 metres long and were unrolled a section at a time.

Retail therapy

shop 'til you drop

The Romans liked a good bargain. Prices were not fixed so people would haggle until they had agreed on a deal. Markets were popular and sold fish, meat, fruit and vegetables. Roman shopping was very noisy and streets were often filled with people shouting out their wares!

Roman shoppers had to get up early. Many shops and market-stalls closed at noon.

The world's first shopping centre was in Rome! Trajan's Forum was built on Quirinal Hill in the centre of Rome. It had more than 150 shops together with a main shopping hall.

Shoppers walked a long way to make purchases because goods were sold in different parts of the city.

Wining and dining

fabulous food

HE REALLY NEEDS TO CUT DOWN!

Romans ate very little during the day. They had bread and water for breakfast and the main meal of the day was around 4 p.m. Only the rich could afford to employ a chef with slaves to help him in the kitchen. Ordinary people went to *popinae* (cheap eating houses) for their main meal, or bought snacks from roadside fast-food stalls.

WE'LL PAY EXTRA – WE'RE STARVING!

WE'RE SOLD OUT!

KEBAB IN MY SHOE...

Fast-food stalls were popular and hot snacks of pastries stuffed with spicy meats sold very quickly!

At parties, Romans ate lying down on couches around a table. The Romans enjoyed spicy food, and food with sweet and sour flavours.

Dinner came in three courses, with a main course of meat and fish. Food was served with lots of wine!

Bathing
Roman style!

The Romans went to the public baths to relax. Baths were more than just a place to get clean. Visitors could take part in sports such as wrestling, have a massage or a haircut. They could buy scented oils, read a book, eat a snack or admire works of art in the sculpture gallery!

Bathers went into a hot, dry room where a slave removed dirt from their skin or gave them a massage.

Although the Romans liked bathing, they only visited the baths about once in every nine days!

The Romans didn't use soap to get clean. They covered their skin in olive oil, which was then scraped off with a *strigil* – a scraper made of wood, bone or metal. The olive oil was kept in a small flask.

THE SAUNA ROOM'S A BIT HOT TODAY!

TRY THE JACUZZI, IT'S GREAT!

SPLASH!

YIPPEEEEE!

NOOO!

To cool off, bathers went for a swim in a lukewarm pool. Finally, they jumped into a bracing cold pool!

Dressed to kill

togas and sandals

Romans wore different clothes depending on how important they were. Ordinary people wore plain white togas made from rough material. Government leaders wore white togas with a purple trim. Rich people's robes were made of smooth, fine-quality wool and silk.

I NEED A TAILORED TOGA!

ONE... MORE... LITTLE TUG...

AAAAAGGGH!

Wearing a toga wasn't easy. It had many folds and drapes and was worn like a sheet around the body.

The emperor wore an all-purple toga – a sign of his importance. Moving in a toga was quite difficult!

Most Romans wore lace-up sandals with open toes. Boots with nail-studded soles were also popular.

Centre of an empire

magnificent Rome

Rome was a beautiful city. The main forum, shown here, was a large, open courtyard, used as a market-place. It was surrounded by buildings such as the Colosseum and government offices and law courts. People often came here to meet friends and listen to open-air speeches.

The basilica was similar to a town hall. It was here that people came together for meetings and the building was often used as a court of law. After the rise of Christianity, many basilicas were used as churches.

Market trader

From a small village of wooden huts, Rome grew to be the finest city the world had ever seen.

The Colosseum

Temple

Basilica (town hall)

The forum

More than one million people lived in this exciting place. The Romans went on to conquer a huge empire.

Place your bets!

chariots of fire!

The Romans loved a day at the races. Chariot racing was held at race tracks called circuses. The most famous was the Circus Maximus, which had seating for 250,000 spectators! Twelve chariots took part in a race, each speeding around an 8-kilometre long track. Up to 24 races were held in a day.

DOWN A BIT, LADS.

WE'RE IN A FOR A BIT OF A BUMPY RIDE!

LET'S LOSE THIS IDIOT ON THE NEXT BEND!

BOING! BOING! BOING!

Chariots often collided and overturned. Many horses and charioteers were killed on the track.

Racing rivalries sometimes caused riots! Races were organized into four separate teams. Charioteers wore tunics in their team's colours – red, blue, white or green – and each team had a keen and violent group of fans.

The life of a chariot driver was very glamorous but often short-lived as the sport was so dangerous. The best drivers were idolized by their supporters.

COME ON! MOVE IT, YOU PAIR OF OLD NAGS!

NAGS! WHAT A CHEEK! WE'RE THOROUGHBREDS!

CHEATS! STOP THE RACE! THIS IS **SABOTAGE!**

Chariots were pulled by two or four horses. Sometimes six or eight were used for added excitement.

Soldiers and weapons

life in the army

Roman soldiers were well paid and well cared for. Soldiers were given thorough training in battle skills and troops carried three main weapons – javelins, swords and daggers. Each soldier bought his own set and he looked after them extremely carefully – one day his life might depend on them.

New soldiers trained hard. They practised fencing and javelin-throwing as well as swimming every day.

can you believe it?

Roman soldiers guarding the northern frontiers of Britain kept warm by wearing woollen trousers, like underpants, under their tunics!

Soldiers were given a uniform when they joined the army. Extra clothing or equipment after this had to be paid for out of their wages. They carried shields made of wood and leather and sharp-tipped javelins. Metal helmets protected their heads and chain-mail armour was worn over their bodies.

THAT HURT!

FAIRY CAKES TODAY, LADS.

LIGHT AS A FEATHER!

NO, I DON'T THINK IT'S **THAT** BAD.

BANG! BANG!

Soldiers learned to do everything for themselves – cooking, building and first-aid, as well as fighting!

Work, work, work

slaving away

Not all people in Rome were equal. Slaves had no rights and they couldn't vote. They belonged to their owners just like dogs or horses. Slaves were bought and sold at markets. They couldn't leave their owners or choose what work to do.

WELL ROME WASN'T BUILT IN A DAY!

I'M GROWING MY HAIR!

YEAH, ME TOO!

SNIP! SNIP!

YOU CHANGE HIM! IT'S YOUR TURN!

WAH! WAH!

YOU KNOW DIRTY NAPPIES MAKE ME SICK.

Slaves did everything their owners told them to, from cleaning to babysitting to labouring on farms.

Slaves were sometimes freed as a reward for their loyalty. Some sick or dying owners did this so that their slaves didn't go to a new owner who might treat them badly.

From 73BC to 71BC a slave called Spartacus led a revolt. He ran away to a hideout where 90,000 other slaves joined him.

THANKS FOR YOUR HELP.

IT'S BEEN A PLEASURE.

WHOOSH!

Some freed slaves did very well and set up their own businesses. A few became doctors or chefs.

Worship
Roman style
good gods!

The Romans worshipped many different gods. Families gave offerings of food and wine to their gods every day. These were left beside statues inside temples. Some gods were asked to curse people's enemies. Messages were written on metal or pottery and left at temples in the hope that the gods might read them.

Can you believe it?

Livers of sacrificed animals were examined by priests. If diseased, bad luck was on the way!

Diana was goddess of the Moon, Neptune was god of the sea and Venus was goddess of love.

Diana also guarded wild animals, while Minerva was goddess of war – along with Mars, god of war.

Jupiter, king of the gods, protected Roman lands. His wife, Juno, was worshipped by married women.

Roman know-how

clever clogs!

The Romans were amazing architects. They invented concrete, and discovered how baked clay bricks were stronger than unbaked ones. They found out how to use arches to strengthen walls and designed massive domes for buildings too big to be roofed with wooden beams.

GULP!

THE DONKEY'S EYES ARE GROWING HEAVY.

I'M AN ASS, YOU FOOL!

EASY, MATE!

The Romans believed witchcraft caused illness. Doctors could sew cuts and join broken bones.

Water was carried into Rome through channels and pipes called aqueducts. Most of these pipes were underground, but some were supported on high arches in bridges. The aqueducts gently sloped to make sure there was a steady supply of water. The water came from fresh streams and springs.

Roman builders were highly skilled. They used tools crafted by local metalworkers and carpenters, and materials such as wood and stone were also locally supplied. There are lots of examples of their work still standing in Rome today.

I'M A PLUMBER BY TRADE — BRICKWORK'S NOT MY THING!

SPLISH SPLASH SPLOSH!

PLUMBER! HAVE SOME WATER THEN!

HEE! HEE!

Aqueducts were pipes set into bridges. They supplied the city with fresh water – for all that bathing!

VIKING INVADERS

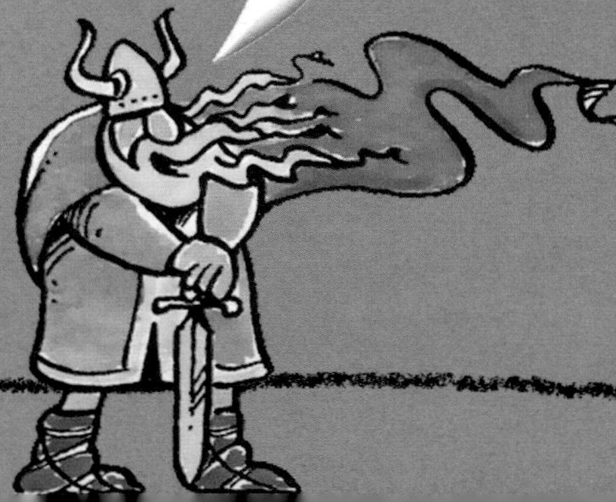

Kings and people

Vikings rule!

The Vikings lived in Scandinavia more than 1000 years ago. They spread terror throughout Europe between AD800 and 1100. Viking warriors made fierce raids on peaceful villages, battled to win new land, plundered treasures and snatched people to sell as slaves.

Slaves, farmers and warriors all worked hard. King Erik Bloodaxe killed his brothers so he could be king.

At the top of Viking society were nobles (kings or chiefs). They were rich and had many servants. The middle group included farmers and craftworkers. Slaves were the lowest group. They worked hard for nobles and could not leave their owner.

Viking rulers had strange names such as Svein Forkbeard, Thorfinn Skullsplitter and Sigurd the stout.

ERM...WHERE'S THE DOOR THEN?

BANG! BANG!

WISH I'D BROUGHT MY SURFBOARD!

King Bluetooth built a memorial for his family. King Cnut tried to command the waves – and failed!

Sailors and raiders
row your boat

Vikings sailed in dragon ships.
Cargo ships were slow and heavy, with wide, deep hulls to carry loads. Ferry and river boats were small and sturdy. The most splendid ships were drakkar (dragon ships), designed for war. They were long, slender and speedy, with beautifully carved sterns and prows.

Dragon ships had shallow keels that enabled the Vikings to sail quickly onto beaches to make raids.

Vikings liked living in longhouses, because heat from the animals provided a kind of central heating, keeping them warm.

Viking pirates such as King Svein Forkbeard of Denmark (ruled AD985–1014) demanded money from the English. He led Viking warships to England and promised to attack if he was not paid to sail away. Svein's tactics worked. Each time he returned, the English handed over 'Dane-geld' (gold for the Danes) – again and again!

Tall trees provided long planks for ships. Vikings used overlapping planks of ash, oak or birch for the hull.

Warriors and weapons
going beserk!

Vikings valued glory over long life. They believed that a dead warrior's fame lived on after him, and made sure that his name would never die. Myths and legends also told how warriors who died in battle would go to Valhalla, home of the gods, for a feasting banquet.

MIRROR MIRROR...

YOU FOOL!

GRRRRR!

EEK!

THEY MUST BE DELIRIOUS, QUICK, RUN!

Berserkirs were fierce warriors who wore animal skins and charged at the enemy, howling like wolves.

Viking kings or lords led their followers into battle. Their men won praise for their loyalty.

Warrior spirits went to Valhalla, home of the gods. They named their swords and were buried with them.

Women and children
ruling the roost

Viking women were very independent. They made important household decisions, cooked, made clothes, raised children, organized slaves and managed farms and workshops while their husbands were away.

Women worked hard at looking after their families. Only widows could marry who they chose to.

If a man wanted to marry, he had to ask the woman's father for permission and pay him a bride price. The marriage went ahead, even if the woman did not agree. All women had the right to ask for a divorce if they were badly treated.

The Vikings imported boatloads of broken glass to melt and recycle into glass beads.

IT'LL END IN TEARS!

OI! SLACKER

MUM, I'VE CHANGED MY MIND ABOUT WOODWORK CLASSES...

WHACK!

Old women won respect for advice. Viking children did not go to school, but learned from their parents.

Skilled craftworkers
tools of the trade

Vikings made most of the things they needed. Families had to make – and mend – almost everything – from their houses and furniture to farm carts, children's toys and clothes. They had no machines to help them, so most of this work was done slowly and carefully by hand.

Blacksmiths travelled around, making and mending tools. Bones were carved into combs by craftworkers.

To make a brooch, silversmiths hammered a die (a block of metal marked with a brooch design) into a sheet of silver. Then they added detail such as filigree (drops of molten silver) and nielo (a black paste).

Traders bought and sold goods using pieces of silver, which they weighed out on silver scales.

OH, YOU SHOULDN'T HAVE!

I DIDN'T!

I FEEL LIKE ONE OF THE SEVEN DWARFS!

BANG

Silversmiths made necklaces from twisted silver wires. Stoneworkers carved cups and bowls from cliffs.

Viking towns

getting settled

Kings built towns to encourage more trade. Before the Vikings grew so powerful, merchants traded at fairs held just once or twice a year. Viking kings built towns so that trade could continue all year round. Taxes were collected from the people and merchants who traded there.

Traders swapped goods, or paid for them using bits of silver, which were later developed into coins.

Towns were targets for attack. Pirates and raiders from Russia and north Germany sailed across the Baltic Sea to snatch valuable goods from Viking towns. So kings paid for towns to be defended with high banks of earth and strong wooden walls.

The name 'Russia' comes from the word 'Rus' used by people living east of the Baltic Sea to describe Viking settlers.

WE'RE COMING TO GET YOU!

SWEAT!

QUICK! LEG IT!

HE'S SUCH A DRAMA QUEEN!

Space was limited inside town walls, which were defended by troops of warriors.

Vikings
at home
family life

Vikings lived in a harsh environment, with cold, long, dark winters. Buildings were needed to shelter livestock, as well as people. In parts of the countryside, farmers built longhouses, with rooms for the family at one end and for animals at the other.

Wooden rafters

outside lavatory

Houses did not have windows so were often full of smoke, making Vikings prone to chest diseases.

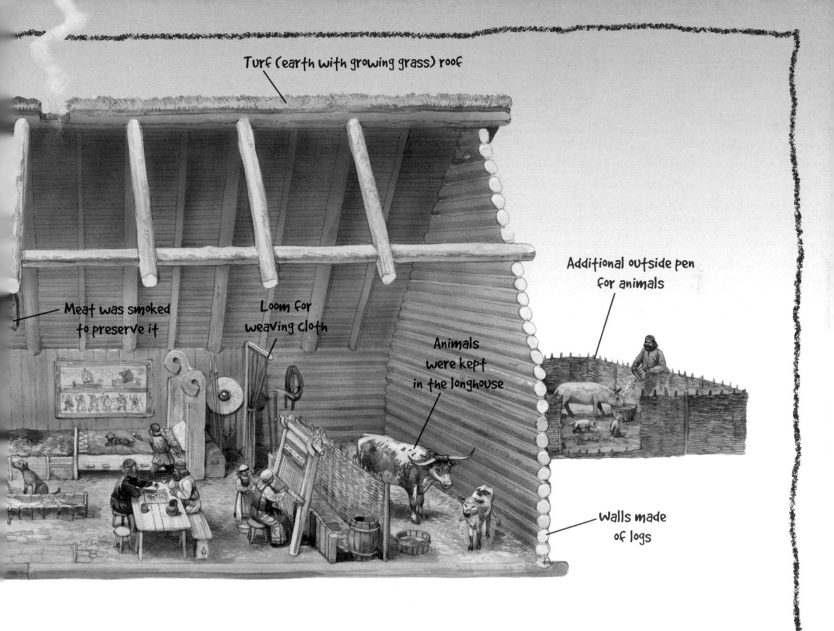

Turf (earth with growing grass) roof

Meat was smoked to preserve it

Loom for weaving cloth

Additional outside pen for animals

Animals were kept in the longhouse

Walls made of logs

Longhouses were built on sloping ground so that animal waste ran downhill, away from living areas.

Time for dinner

fun of the feast!

Vikings ate two meals a day. First thing in the morning was the 'day meal' of barley bread or oatcakes, butter or cheese. The main meal – 'night meal' – was eaten in the early evening. It included meat or fish, plus wild berries in summer. Meals were served on wooden plates or soapstone bowls and eaten with metal knives and wood or horn spoons.

Viking women and slaves cooked huge meals over open fires and served them to feasting warriors.

Red-hot stones boiled water for cooking. Few Viking homes had ovens so women and servants boiled meat in iron cauldrons. They also used water-filled pits that were heated by stones that had been placed in fire to make them red-hot. This was a very efficient way of cooking.

Feasts went on for a week or more. After winning a great victory, Vikings liked to celebrate. Kings and lords held feasts to reward their warriors, and families feasted at weddings. Guests dressed in their best clothes and hosts provided much food and drink. Everyone stayed in the feast hall until the food ran out, or they grew tired.

WHOOSH!

WHERE AM I? HIC!

BORING!

ENTERTAINMENT'S TERRIBLE!

Viking warriors drank from curved cattle horns, but most people drank from wooden or pottery beakers.

Law and order

keeping the peace

Vikings followed a strict code of honour. Men and women were proud and dignified, and honour was important to them. It was a disgrace to be called a cheat or a coward, or to run away from a fight. Vikings also prized loyalty. They swore solemn promises to be faithful to lords and comrades and sealed bargains by shaking hands.

SULK? ME? NEVER!

WHOOSH!

BANG!

DING! DING! ROUND THREE

TAKE THAT!

Quarrels were settled by fighting and this often lead to family feuds that lasted for months.

Viking laws were not written down. Instead, they were memorized by a man known as the law-speaker. He recited the laws out loud every year so that everyone could hear and understand them.

Every year Vikings met at the Thing – a gathering of all free men where they discussed punishments for prisoners.

GO ON, SHAKE ON IT...

COME ON, LET'S ALL BE FRIENDS AGAIN.

...IT WAS THIS BIG! HONEST!

FOR MY NEXT TRICK...

HUMPH!

Feuding families eventually had to call a truce. Viking thieves were hanged or outlawed.

Having a laugh

relaaax!

Vikings liked to have a good time. At feasts, people sang songs and danced. When relaxing, Vikings often played dice and board games. They loved playing practical jokes too, and listening to stories about gods and heroes who defeated enemies by trickery.

ALTOGETHER NOW!

A Viking feast included lots of food, drink and dancing. A feast could go on for several days!

Vikings had a good sense of humour, and they liked jokes. In summer they played games and ran races.

Acrobats and jugglers were popular at feasts. Sports such as archery were good training for war.

Gods...
and goddesses

Viking people honoured many gods. The Aesir (sky gods) included Odin, Thor and Tyr, who were gods of war, and Loki, who was a trickster. The Vanir (gods of earth and water) included Njord (god of the sea) and Frey (the farmers' god). He and his sister Freyja brought pleasure and fertility.

Thor, god of thunder, travelled in a chariot pulled by goats. Odin god of war, rode an eight-legged horse.

The Vikings believed that they could win favours from the gods by offering them gifts. Since life was the most valuable gift, they gave the gods sacrifices of animals – and people.

one story told how Viking god Thor dressed up as a bride and pretended to marry a giant who had stolen his golden hammer.

WHAT A DRIP!

FREE ENTRY FOR SPIRITS!

VALHALLA HERE WE COME, BOYS!

Njord was the sea god. Warrior spirits went to live with the goddess Freyja, or Valhalla, home of the gods.

Death and burial
a good send off

The dead took useful items with them to the next world. The Vikings believed that peoples' souls survived to go on living in the next world. The bodies of the dead were surrounded by 'grave goods' – all kinds of things they might need such as clothes, weapons and jewellery.

I'M NO ANGEL!

SHE WAS SUCH A NICE LADY!

SNIFF!

A TRUE DIAMOND!

SNIFF

BUT THAT'S MY FAVOURITE SHIELD IN THERE, NOT HIS!

Vikings burned their dead on fires and collected the ashes. From AD800, unburned bodies were buried.

Can you believe it?

Some Viking skeletons that were buried in acid soil have been eaten away but have left shadows in the ground.

Vikings treated dead bodies with respect. They washed them, dressed them and wrapped them in cloth or birch bark before burying them or cremating them. This was because the Vikings believed that dead people might come back to haunt them if they were not treated carefully.

BON VOYAGE!

RIGHT, I'M OFF BEFORE SEA-SICKNESS SETS IN!

Sometimes, the dead were laid to rest in cloth-covered shelters on board ships that were set on fire.

End
of an era

Norman invasions

Kings defeated the Vikings.

For centuries, kings in England, Scotland and Ireland failed to drive the Vikings from their lands. But after AD1000, they began to succeed. Brian Boru, high king of Ireland, defeated the Vikings in 1014, and Viking rule ended in England in 1042.

In 1066 the Normans (descendants of Vikings) invaded from Normandy, France, and conquered England.

Vikings learned to live alongside other peoples. In most places where they settled, Vikings married local women and worked with local people. Some of their words and customs blended with local ones, but many simply disappeared.

After AD1000, Viking settlers landed in America, but the Native Americans drove them away.

A castle was both a home and a fortress in the Middle Ages. It provided shelter for a king or a lord and his family, and allowed him to defend his lands. Castles were also places where soldiers were stationed, wrong-doers were imprisoned, courts settled disputes, weapons were made and banquets and tournaments were held.

Wooden castles were not very strong and burnt down easily, so stone castles were built from the 1100s.

The first castles were mostly built from wood on top of a hill called a motte. On the motte stood a wooden tower, or keep. This was the central part of the castle and the easiest area to defend.

The builders of early wooden castles covered the walls with wet leather to protect them from fire.

Stone castles were stronger and gave better protection from attack, fire and the weather.

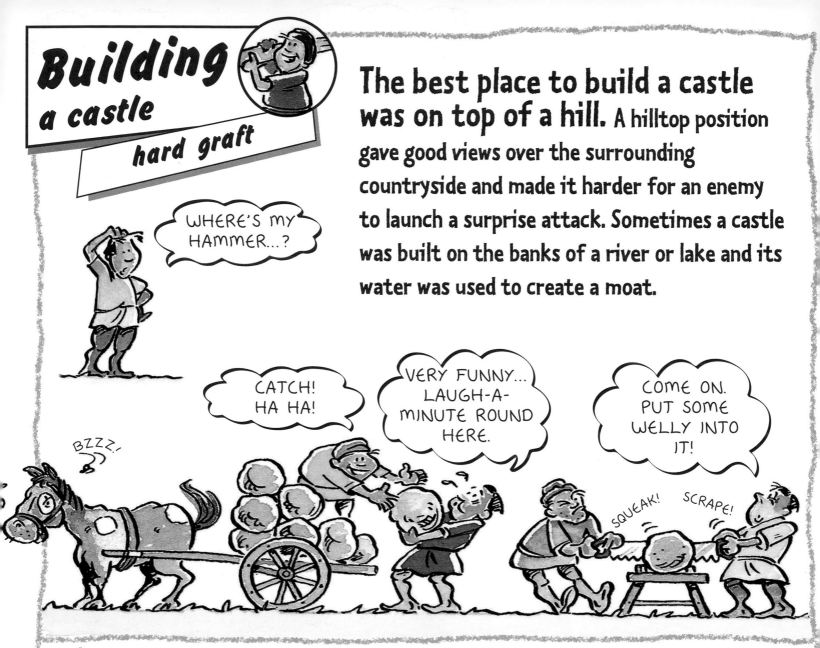

Building a castle

hard graft

The best place to build a castle was on top of a hill. A hilltop position gave good views over the surrounding countryside and made it harder for an enemy to launch a surprise attack. Sometimes a castle was built on the banks of a river or lake and its water was used to create a moat.

WHERE'S MY HAMMER...?

CATCH! HA HA!

VERY FUNNY... LAUGH-A-MINUTE ROUND HERE.

COME ON. PUT SOME WELLY INTO IT!

BZZZ!

SQUEAK!

SCRAPE!

Building a castle involved hundreds of workers, from labourers to stone masons and carpenters.

The planning and design of the castle were managed by a mason. Supplies were brought in by river.

The lord of the castle lived in the keep, the safest part of the castle. Its thick walls were well-guarded.

Castle capers

who's who?

A castle was the home of an important and powerful person, such as a king, a lord or a knight. The lord of the castle controlled the castle itself, as well as the lands and people around it. The lady of the castle was in charge of the day-to-day running of things. She controlled the kitchens and gave the servants their orders for feasts and banquets.

YOU LOOK A BIT SHEEPISH!

YAWN

WAKEY WAKEY!

SLEEPING ON THE JOB?

CAN'T GET THE STAFF THESE DAYS.

SPLISH!

Servants lived and worked inside the castle, cooking, cleaning and serving food to the lord and his family.

There was no bathroom for the servants. They had to take a dip in the local river to wash — and get rid of any fleas and lice!

The constable was in charge of defending the castle. He trained his soldiers to guard the castle properly and he organized a rota of guards and watchmen. When the lord was away, the constable was in charge of the entire castle.

I WANT MY DINNER AND I WANT IT **NOW!**

TEMPER TEMPER!

WHAT'S HE **BANG**ING ON ABOUT?

BANG!

Inside the castle walls were workshops where important tools and weapons were made and repaired.

King of the castle

In medieval times, the king or queen was the most important person in the country. The king gave land to his barons and other noblemen. In return, they supplied the king with soldiers, horses and weapons to fight wars. This system of giving away land in return for services was known as feudalism.

The Church was powerful in the Middle Ages, and it grew rich from charging peasants to live on its land.

Barons were the most powerful noblemen – they supplied the king with men who would fight.

At the bottom of the feudal system were peasants. Everything they owned belonged to the local lord.

Good knight!

how to be one

It took about 14 years of training to become a knight. The son of a noble joined a lord's household at the age of seven. There he learned how to ride, to shoot a bow and arrow and how to behave in front of nobles. He then became a squire and learned how to fight with a sword.

LOVE ME, LOVE MY HORSE!

ARISE, SIR KNIGHT!

WHERE'S YOUR FIGHTING **SPIRIT**! WHOOOO!

Men were knighted in a dubbing ceremony. The night before the ceremony was spent praying in church.

A knight who behaved badly was disgraced and punished. He may have behaved in a cowardly way on the battlefield, cheated in a tournament or treated another knight badly.

A French knight sent love poems to the Countess of Tripoli, even though he had never met her. When he finally saw her he fell into her arms and died.

YAHOOO!

IT'S HARDLY ROCKET SCIENCE IS IT!

BOING!

PUFF

KILL THE ENEMY! CHAAARGE!

BOYS, BOYS, WE'RE ONLY PRACTISING!

EEK!

Knights followed a code of chivalry. This involved being brave in battle and treating the enemy fairly.

Battle fashion
keeping safe

Knights wore tunics made of linen or wool, with a cloak over the top. By the 1200s, knights had started to wear long, hooded coats called surcoats. Knights wore bright colours, and some even wore fancy items such as shoes with curled, pointed toes and hats decorated with jewels.

Gradually knights began to wear more and more armour. They even wore metal gloves and shoes!

Soldiers called 'retrievers' had to run into the middle of the battle and collect all the spare arrows!

Early knights wore a type of armour called chainmail. It was made of thousands of tiny iron rings joined together. A piece of chainmail looked a bit like knitting, except it was made of metal, not wool. A knight also wore a padded jacket under his chainmail to make sure he wasn't cut by his own armour!

W H O O S H !

CLUMP!

TEA FOR TWO!

TAKE THAT, YOU WALKING TIN CAN! HEE HEE!

England and France were at war between 1337 and 1453. This long dispute was called the Hundred Years War.

Inside a castle

dingy dungeons

Castles had no central heating and no running water. Wool hangings and tapestries on the walls helped to keep the rooms warm. Roaring fires burned in huge fireplaces.

The centre of activity was the great hall. This was where banquets and important meetings were held. In the kitchens, meat sizzled on spits in front of the fire. The bedrooms were cold and draughty. Fresh reeds covered the floors as there were no carpets.

Almost all castles had a well within their walls. This was an essential water source in a siege.

Castle key

1. **Gatehouse** – the tower and gates that guard the entrance to a castle.
2. **Great hall** – the big business room that was used for banquets and feasts.
3. **Portcullis** – a heavy metal fence that sealed off the castle gateway.
4. **Tower** – a tall building from which enemies could be seen.
5. **Machicolations** – small chutes from which missiles could be dropped on the enemy.
6. **Battlements** – walkways that were defended by stone blocks.
7. **Arrow loops** – narrow slits in the walls through which archers could fire arrows.

Every castle had a cold, dark, slimy dungeon for holding prisoners, who were locked in smelly cells.

Feasts and fun

boozy banquets

The great hall was the centre of castle life. The lord and his family ate their meals here and carried out their daily business. Colourful banners, coats-of-arms and shiny pieces of armour hung from the walls. The hall was sometimes turned into a courtroom to try law-breakers.

ROWDY LOT!

YUMMY!

GLUG

FILL ME UP, WENCH

IS THIS ORGANIC?

NO, IT'S CHICKEN!

Jesters, jugglers and sometimes even a dancing bear performed for the diners between courses.

can you believe it?

The Turks fought with gold pieces in their mouths to stop the crusader knights from stealing it.

The lord, his family and important guests sat at the high table on a platform called a dais. From their raised position they could look down over the rest of the diners. The most important guests such as priests and noblemen sat next to the lord.

Huge amounts of exotic-looking food were served at banquets. Roast meats were very popular.

Knights and dragons

fiery fables

The legend of St George tells how a brave knight killed a fierce dragon. The dragon was terrorizing the people of Lydia (part of modern Turkey).

The king of Lydia even offered his daughter to the dragon if it promised to leave them alone.

George killed the dragon and the people of Lydia became Christians. St George is the patron saint of England.

A crusader knight would share his tent with his beloved horse – it must have been a bit of a squeeze!

King Arthur had many castle homes but his favourite was Camelot. Historians think that Camelot was really an English castle called Tintagel. No one really knows who the real Arthur was but he may have been a Celtic warrior who lived 1400 years ago.

MERLIN, IT'S NOT AS EASY AS IT LOOKS...

MATE, THAT SWORD IS STUCK.

CALL YOURSELF A KNIGHT! WIMP!

POOR BOY!

Legend says that King Arthur became king after pulling a magic sword, called Excalibur, from a stone.

Practice for battle

play fights

COME ON! GIVE IT SOME!

In a tournament, knights divided into two sides and fought each other as if in a real battle. Tournaments were good practice for the real thing – war. The idea for these mock battles, called tourneys, probably started in France in the 12th century.

READY TO RUMBLE?

READY TO TUMBLE?

WHOA!

Jousting knights charged with a long pole called a lance. Each tried to knock his opponent off his horse.

Jousting was introduced because so many knights were being killed or wounded during tournaments. Jousting knights were protected by armour and their lances were not sharp.

Some knights cheated in jousts by wearing special armour that was fixed onto the horse's saddle!

Sometimes knights would carry on fighting on the ground with their swords, but this was dangerous.

Castle
under siege
chaaaaarge!

An attacking enemy had to break through a castle's defences to get inside its walls. One way was to break down the castle gates with battering rams. Attackers and defenders also used siege engines to hurl boulders at each other.

Giant catapults were used to fire stones or burning pieces of wood at the castle.

The ropes used to wind up siege catapults were made from plaits of human hair!

A siege engine called a trebuchet had a long wooden arm with a heavy weight at one end and a sling at the other. A big stone was placed in the sling, and as the weight dropped, the stone was hurled towards the castle walls, sometimes travelling as far as 300 metres.

WHOOSH!

PUUSH!

WE ARE!

YOU COULD TRY KNOCKING!

Soldiers charged with huge, heavy battering rams to smash down castle gates.

Castle defences
keeping safe

When enemies were spotted approaching a castle, its defenders pulled up the castle drawbridge. They also lowered an iron grate, called a portcullis, to form an extra barrier behind the drawbridge.

COOOEE!

YOU'RE SUPPOSED TO BOIL THE WATER FIRST...

FOOL! YOU GIVE US ARROWS, NOT FLOG 'EM!

I WANT MY MUM!

Defenders poured boiling water onto the heads of the enemy as they tried to climb the castle walls.

The castle archers fired their arrows through gaps in the battlements and slits in the castle walls.

In the night a group from inside the castle would sometimes surprise the attackers outside.

PLUNDERING PIRATES

Terror from the sea
pirate attack

A pirate is a robber on the sea. Pirates attack ships and ports, stealing treasure and other goods. The Greek islands were home to some of the earliest pirates. Around 500BC, there were many ships trading along the Mediterranean coasts. They were easy prey for the pirates.

Early pirates stole amber, copper and silver and stashed it away on their island hideouts.

In 67BC, the Roman leader Pompey wanted to stop pirates stealing Rome's food supplies.

Viking invaders raided the British coast. Even Julius Caesar was captured by pirates – but then released.

Caught by corsairs

kidnapped!

ANOTHER FINE MESS WE'RE IN!

Pirates of the Mediterranean were known as 'corsairs'. They hunted people, not treasure. Corsairs sold ordinary captives as slaves or forced them to work in their galleys. Richer people were more valuable. The two most feared corsairs were the Barbarossa brothers. They lived during the 16th century.

Galley slaves were forced to row the big heavy oars. They were chained together at the ankle.

In 1816, a fleet of English and Dutch ships attacked a group of corsairs near Algiers on the North African coast. The corsairs were forced to release over 3000 slaves.

The Barbarossa brothers were so-called because of their beards.
Barbarossa means 'Redbeard' in Latin.

Some slaves tried to escape by land, whilst others risked the dangers at sea. Very few got away.

Trail of treasure
across the sea

From the early 1500s, Spanish galleons carried vast amounts of treasure across the Atlantic. Loaded with American gold, silver, jewels and other riches, these big vessels were heavily armed. But they were also slow and heavy, and attracted pirates like bees to a honeypot.

Francis le Clerc was a fierce pirate who had a wooden leg. He captured Havana in Cuba and set it alight.

Soldiers guarding the Spanish treasure were called 'conquistadors'. They were the first of the Spanish soldiers to invade South America. Conquistadors often travelled with the treasure ships, but were no real match for the pirates.

Spanish galleons sailed in groups to protect themselves from pirate attack.

Wily sea dogs
serving the Queen

John Hawkins made many raids on treasure ships in the Spanish Main. However, he did not call himself a pirate. He carried a letter from Queen Elizabeth I of England, which allowed him to attack ships from an enemy nation. Hawkins, and many like him, were called 'privateers'.

THREE POUNDS WHAT?

SEE YA!

YOU CAN'T JUST WALK ON BOARD!

CAN! IT'S WRITTEN HERE IN BLACK AND WHITE!

Hawkin's letter allowed him to attack any ship – he became very rich.

Drake risked death by raiding a treasure store but when the store was opened, it was empty!

Francis Drake was the greatest of the Elizabethan 'sea dogs'. He first went to sea at 14, and later joined his cousin John Hawkins on his expeditions. Like Hawkins, he became a privateer, and carried on an unofficial war against Spain.

DONKEYS, MA'AM.

WE'RE MULES! YOU FOOL!

FRANCIS, I LOVE THIS BLING THING!

BLING!

In 1572, Drake ambushed a mule train laden with treasure, which he gave to the Queen.

All aboard!

life at sea

Most pirate ships had to be small and fast. On the Spanish Main, many were 'schooners', with two masts. The captain's cabin was in the stern (back), while the crew slept in the middle of the ship. Treasure, gunpowder and food were kept in the hold.

Below deck it was cramped, smelly and noisy. Pirates barely had room to put up their hammocks.

Most pirates dressed like other sailors of the time. They wore short blue jackets, checked shirts and baggy canvas trousers. However, some showed off the finery they had stolen, such as velvet trousers, black felt hats, silk shirts and crimson waistcoats with gold buttons and lace.

In calm weather, there was little for the pirates to do. They would mend ropes and sails, or gamble with dice. In bad weather, or when they were chasing another ship, life was very busy. The crew might have to climb aloft in the rigging to alter the sails, keep lookout from high on the mainmast, or prepare the cannon for firing.

Fresh food was hard to come by on board a ship, so the cook served dry biscuits and pickled meat.

Women pirates

dressed to kill

Grace O'Malley commanded a pirate fleet on Ireland's west coast. She went to sea as a young girl, and later moved into a stone castle on the coast. Her fleet of sailing ships attacked passing vessels. In 1593, Grace begged Queen Elizabeth for a pardon. She lived to be over 70 years old.

Anne Bonny and Mary Read were braver than their male crew, who hid rather than fight the British!

can you believe it?

Grace o'Malley cut her hair short to look like her sailors. They all nicknamed her baldy!

One of the greatest women pirates was Ching Shih. When her husband died in 1807, she took over his raiding fleet on the Chinese coast. She was a brilliant leader and forced her sailors to obey a strict set of rules.

Ching Shih was said to feed her captives on just caterpillars and rice.

Hunting the pirates

navy power

Edward Teach was the most terrifying pirate on the seas. He was better known as Blackbeard.

European countries started to build bigger and stronger navies. With these, they were able to begin ridding the sea of pirates. Well-armed navy fleets patrolled the trouble spots. Pirates were offered free pardons if they gave up their lives of crime.

Large rewards were given to anyone who helped to capture pirate ships, but it was a dangerous task.

Blackbeard made himself look as frightening as possible by plaiting ribbons in his beard and putting lighted matches under his hat. One man was not afraid of Blackbeard – naval officer Robert Maynard.

In 1718, Maynard cornered Blackbeard. He leapt aboard his ship and fought him to the death.

Shiver me timbers!
the jolly roger

When a pirate captain decided to attack, he raised a special flag. Not every pirate flag was the famous skull-and-crossbones. Most early pirates used a bright red flag to frighten their victims. Black flags became popular in the early 1700s, with pirates adding their own symbols.

Once aboard, the pirates would have a bloody fight – often the merchants would simply surrender.

Merchants often hid their cargo. The pirates had to search everywhere and tear apart walls and doors to find it. They might even torture their captives until they told them where it was hidden.

Can you believe it?

Bartholomew Roberts was probably the most successful pirate ever. He never drank anything stronger than tea!

JUST THOUGHT I'D DROP IN!

I'LL STAY UP HERE, THANKS.

I'M A BAREFOOT BANDIT!

I'D RATHER WALK THE PLANK!

Pirates threw ropes with hooks on the end at the enemies' sails, and used them to climb aboard.

131

Pirate plunder
pieces of eight

All pirates dreamed of gold and silver. Some were lucky enough to capture ships packed with silver coins, gold bars or finely made ornaments. However most merchant ships carried humbler goods, such as cloth, coal or iron.

The captain shared the loot amongst his crew. He did this very carefully so no one complained.

Pirates also needed everyday things. If they had been away from land for several weeks, they would be glad to steal food, drink and other provisions. Fresh guns, cannon balls and gunpowder always came in useful!

one of the most valuable cargoes of all was spices from India and Sri Lanka!

SO, HOW MUCH DO **YOU** THINK YOU'RE WORTH?

WELL, I'M WORTH MORE THAN HIM!

POLLY... LOTS OF LOLLY!

SQUAWK!

BLING!

BLING!

Pirates would hold a rich person captive, and demand a ransom. 'Pieces of eight' were used as currency.

Buried treasure

x marks the spot

Pirates hid their treasure by burying it in a remote spot.

Many believe that William Kidd buried a vast store before he was captured. His piracy had gained him a huge amount of cargo, most of which he sold or gave to his crew. When he was arrested in 1699, Kidd claimed he had hidden £100,000 of treasure.

Pirates drew maps of where they buried their treasure so that they would be able to find it again.

After attacking a mule train, Francis Drake found that his ships had sailed away. He ordered his men to bury the loot. Then he made a raft, paddled out to find his ships, and brought them back. Drake then dug up the treasure and put it on board.

There was no code of conduct between pirates, so they would steal treasure from each other, too.

Desert islands
marooned!

Some pirate captains had strict rules. 'Black Bart' Roberts made his crew promise to keep to a code of conduct. They could not gamble or fight on board ship, or keep lights and candles burning after 8 o'clock at night. Anyone who brought a woman on board, or who deserted the ship, would be put to death or marooned.

The Pacific islands were mainly uninhabited, so castaways used their wits to survive.

Marooning was a terrible fate. The pirate was left alone on a deserted island while his friends sailed away. He was given a few vital things but it was almost impossible to escape, and food was hard to find.

Alexander Selkirk was stranded on a desert island off the coast of Chile in 1704. He survived there for five years!

SOB! BUT I MISS MY MUM!

FLAMIN' SHARKS THINK THEY OWN THE PLACE!

Sometimes pirates would even maroon their captain! Many castaways did not survive for long.

Crime and... punishment

Many captured pirates were shipped back to Britain in chains. But most never got that far. They were taken to the nearest American port and executed as quickly as possible. Only the younger criminals were pardoned and released.

YOU'VE BEEN VERY NAUGHTY BOYS!

YOU'RE A BUNCH OF CROOKS AND THAT'S THAT!

YOU WHIFF, MATE!

LET US GO AND WE'LL TELL YOU WHERE OUR TREASURE IS!

Before and after trial, the pirates were kept in prisons that were foul, smelly and overcrowded.

Judges were keen to condemn pirates as quickly as possible, so that any still at large would be scared.

Pirates that were found guilty were hanged. As a warning to others, their bodies were put on display.

Index

Index

Index

Index

Index